Tell Me WHY

Technology

Questions and Answers

by
Rebecca Phillips-Bartlett

Minneapolis, Minnesota

Credits
All images are courtesy of Shutterstock.com, unless otherwise specified. With thanks to Getty Images, Thinkstock Photo, and iStockphoto.

Cover – BNP Design Studio, alexdndz, Devita ayu silvianingtyas, Ilya Bolotov, Incomible, masmas, miniaria, my.ordinarty, Net Vector, pixssa, Ramy Fathalla, Tartila, Orgus88. Throughout – BNP Design Studio, Orgus88, Natalia Sheinkin, Ali Designer 20, Nattapol_Sritongcom, Aliva, Perfectorius. 4–5 – sihuo0860371, alptraum, vetkit. 6–7 – Colorfuel Studio, trgrowth, YUCALORA, BNP Design Studio, Pro_Vector, SDI Productions, forest_strider, skegbydave, designer29. 8–9 – Lakeview Images, vasabii, octopusaga. 10–11 – GoodStudio, judyjump, Far700, Diabluses. 12–13 – Irina Strelnikova, Katja.Vary, janrysavy, 3dgoksu. 14–15 – AnyaPL, ace03, grinvalds. 16–17 – ONYXprj, Solonesafe, iProPav, rjp85, DonNichols, thomasd007. 18–19 – thanya, Nadzin, solar22, AlexandrBognat. 20–21 – Colorfuel Studio, Tenstudio, LSOphoto, eliflamra. 22–23 –Urilux, pagadesign, Waeel Quttene.

Bearport Publishing Company Product Development Team
Publisher: Jen Jenson; Director of Product Development: Spencer Brinker; Managing Editor: Allison Juda; Editor: Cole Nelson; Associate Editor: Naomi Reich; Associate Editor: Tiana Tran; Art Director: Colin O'Dea; Designer: Kim Jones; Designer: Kayla Eggert; Product Development Specialist: Owen Hamlin

Library of Congress Cataloging-in-Publication Data is available at www.loc.gov or upon request from the publisher.

ISBN: 979-8-89232-757-2 (hardcover)
ISBN: 979-8-89232-953-8 (paperback)
ISBN: 979-8-89232-844-9 (ebook)

© 2025 BookLife Publishing
This edition is published by arrangement with BookLife Publishing.

North American adaptations © 2025 Bearport Publishing Company. All rights reserved. No part of this publication may be reproduced in whole or in part, stored in any retrieval system, or transmitted in any form or by any means, electronic, mechanical, photocopying, recording, or otherwise, without written permission from the publisher.

For more information, write to Bearport Publishing, 5357 Penn Avenue South, Minneapolis, MN 55419.

Contents

TELL ME WHY

Our world is full of incredible technology. From computers to cars, people use many kinds of tech every single day.

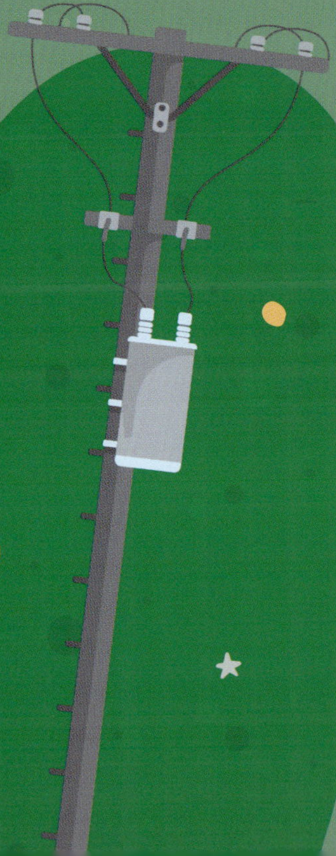

QUESTION
What questions do you have about technology?

We solve many problems with technology. Phones let us stay in touch with people we care about. Cars help us get from place to place. These inventions are amazing, but there are so many things about technology that leave us wondering **WHY?**

WHY IS THE INTERNET IMPORTANT?

The internet is important because it gives people around the world easy access to information, ideas, and stories. Many people use it for their jobs or school.

The internet also keeps the world connected. It allows people to communicate through messages and video calls.

WHY DO I NEED STRONG PASSWORDS?

Passwords help protect your information. The **devices**, websites, and apps that require passwords often store personal information, such as your name and birthday. Strong passwords prevent other people from signing in to your accounts and getting your information.

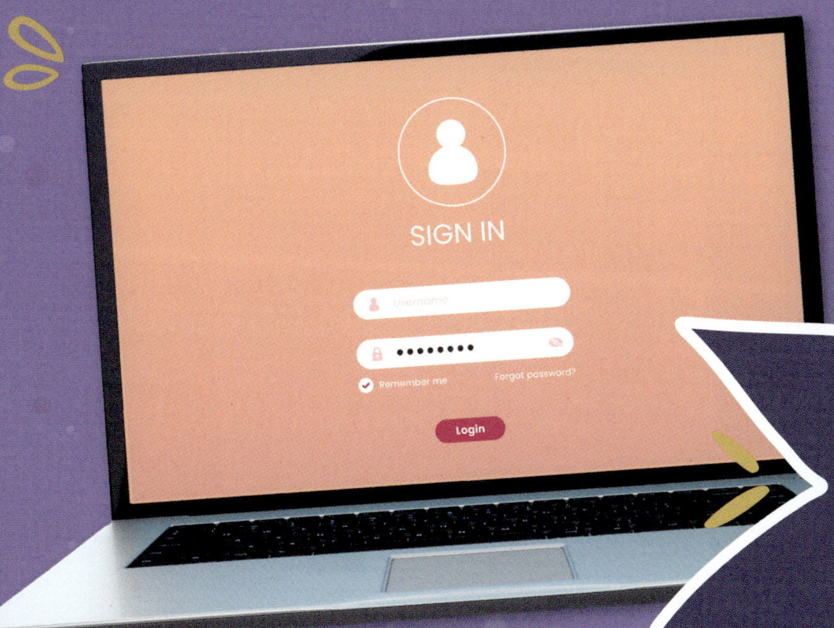

FUN FACT

Strong passwords are hard to guess. They often include letters, numbers, and symbols.

WHY ARE LETTERS ON KEYBOARDS IN A STRANGE ORDER?

Before computers, typewriters became a common way for people to write messages. Each key on a typewriter was attached to a tiny hammer that swung up and stamped the letter onto the page. The first typewriters had the letter keys arranged in alphabetical order, but there was a problem.

When someone quickly typed letters that were near each other, the hammers got stuck together. To fix this problem, the keys were rearranged so that common letter pairings were spread across the keyboard.

FUN FACT

The common English keyboard layout is called QWERTY. These are the first six letters of the keys in the top row.

WHY DO WE HAVE OVERHEAD POWER LINES?

Power lines carry electricity across long distances. Tall towers keep the **dangerous** cables high above the ground so people can safely move beneath them.

QUESTION

Have you ever noticed power lines above roads or fields?

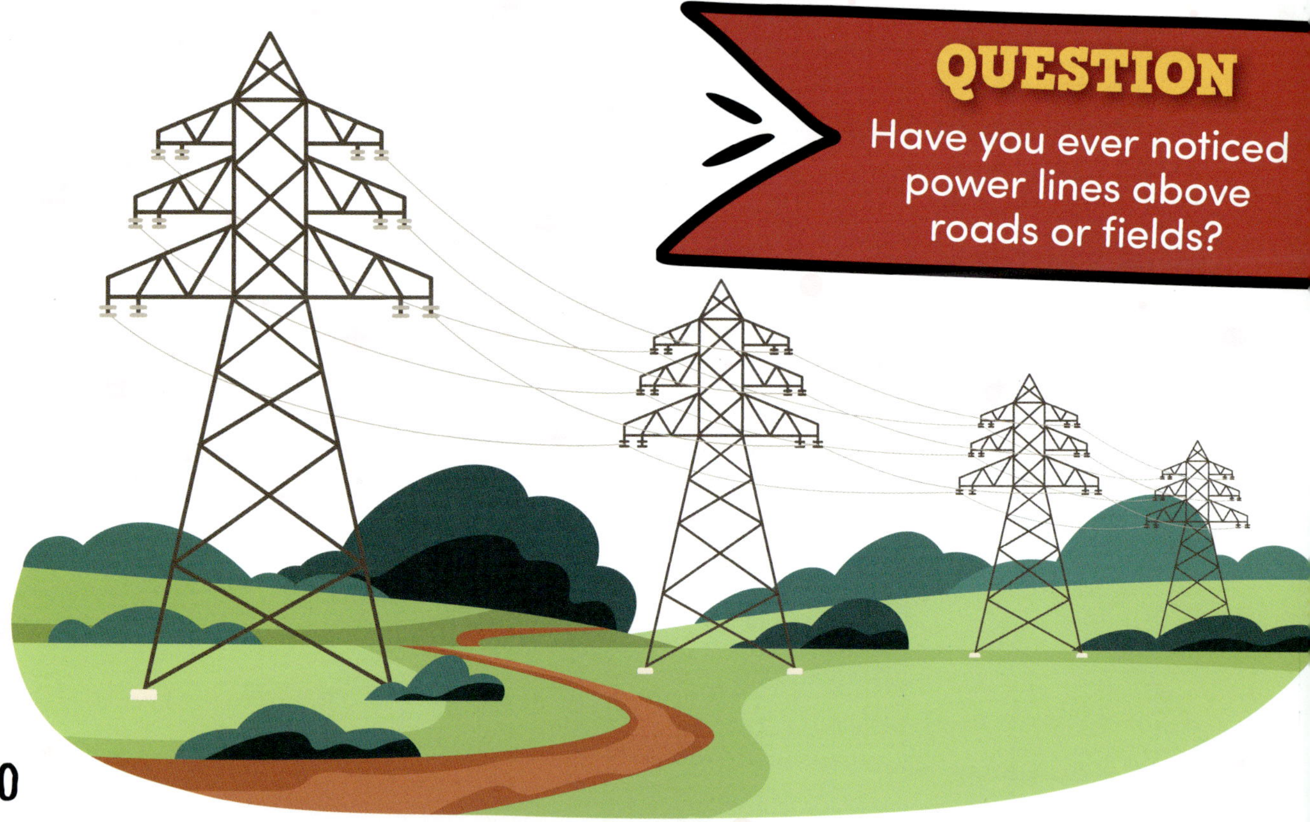

WHY DO POWER OUTAGES HAPPEN?

A power outage happens when there is an interruption in the flow of electricity.

The most common reason for a power outage is **damage** to power lines. This damage is often caused by bad weather.

WHY DO SOME PEOPLE DRIVE ELECTRIC CARS?

Electric cars are powered by batteries. They need electricity to work. Other cars burn **fossil fuels** to power their engines. However, burning these fuels harms the planet. Many people drive electric cars to help save Earth.

Some people drive electric cars because they may save money over time. Electricity is usually cheaper than gas. So, charging the batteries in these cars is less expensive than buying gas for fuel-powered cars.

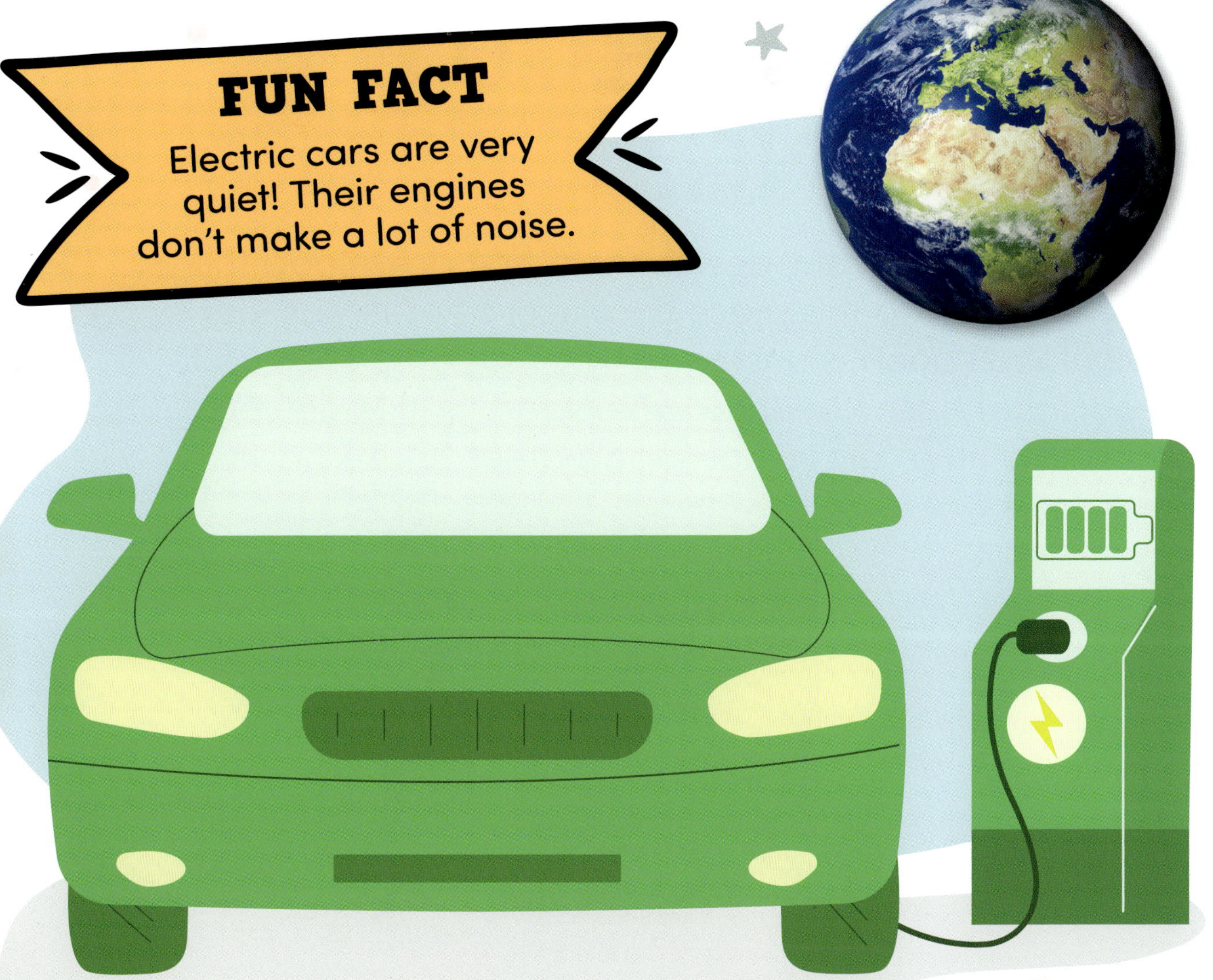

FUN FACT

Electric cars are very quiet! Their engines don't make a lot of noise.

WHY DO ONLINE VIDEOS SOMETIMES STOP WITHOUT WARNING?

To play a video, your device must first download the video. It may do this piece by piece. Sometimes, the download speed is unsteady. The video catches up to a part that hasn't been downloaded, or it is slowed down by the effort to download other future parts.

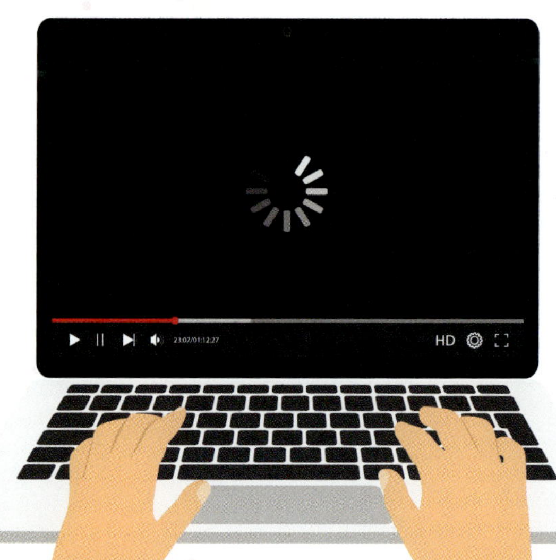

WHY DO SOME DEVICES NEED TO BE CHARGED?

Many devices, such as smartphones and laptops, are powered by batteries. But batteries store a limited amount of **energy**. When you use these devices, it reduces this stored energy. Once the batteries run out of electricity, the devices must be plugged in to recharge.

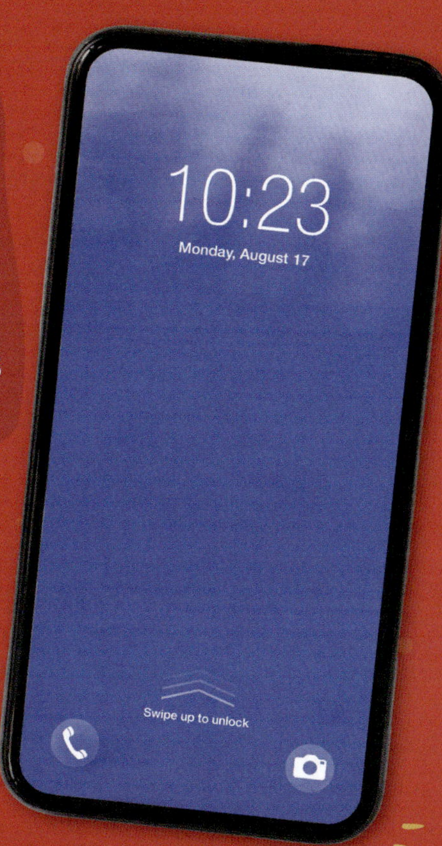

FUN FACT

Some larger devices, such as TVs, do not use batteries. They must be plugged into an electrical **outlet** to work.

WHY ARE ELECTRICAL OUTLETS DIFFERENT AROUND THE WORLD?

There are about 15 different types of electrical outlets around the world. When outlets were being invented, many countries had electrical systems that used different **voltage** levels. Each country made outlets that worked for its own systems. Today, most countries still have the same outlets they first used.

QUESTION

What do the electrical outlets look like in your country?

WHY ARE WIRES DIFFERENT COLORS?

Electrical wires are covered in colored plastic to help tell them apart. Each color has a special meaning that shows what the wire is used for. This helps **electricians** know which wires are safe to handle and which ones could give them a nasty electric shock.

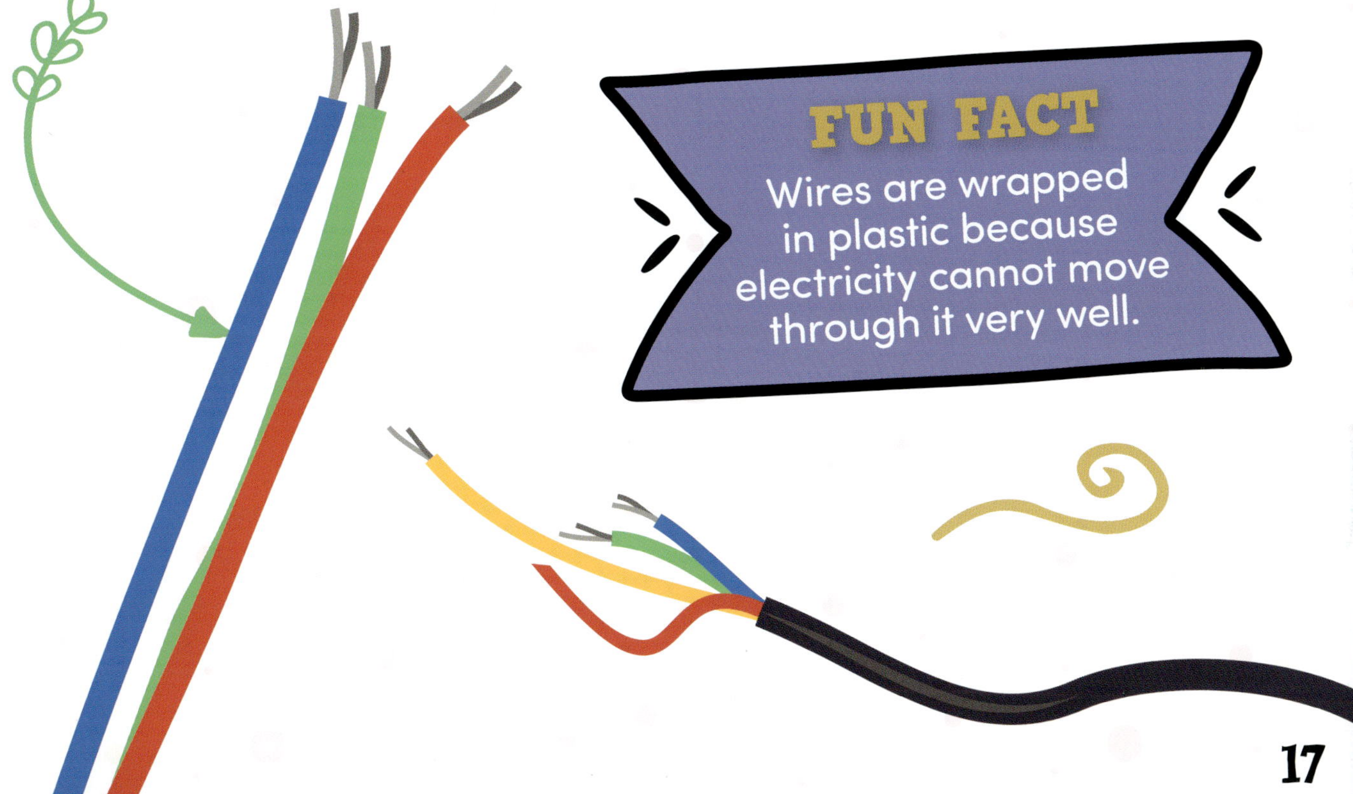

FUN FACT

Wires are wrapped in plastic because electricity cannot move through it very well.

WHY ARE WATER AND ELECTRICITY BAD TOGETHER?

Water and electricity are a dangerous mix. This is because water can easily transport electricity. When electricity touches water, it immediately spreads throughout it. Even a little bit of water can carry a dangerous amount of electricity. If someone touches water that has electricity, they can be **electrocuted**.

Water is also bad for electronic devices. If water gets into a device, electricity spreads quickly and damages parts inside the device.

WHY ARE SCREENS BAD FOR MY EYES?

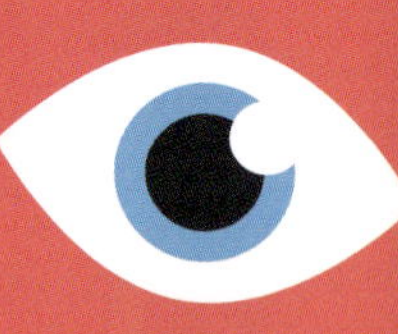

Looking at electronic screens makes your eyes work harder than usual. This is because they are often focusing on what is on the screen for a long time. You may also blink less often while looking at screens. These things cause eye **strain**. This may make your eyes feel dry and tired. It can even give you a headache.

FUN FACT

To prevent eye strain, doctors recommend looking away from your screen every 20 minutes.

WHY SHOULD I AVOID SCREENS BEFORE BED?

How sleepy you feel is controlled by a **hormone** called melatonin. When it is dark outside, your body makes more melatonin to help prepare for sleep.

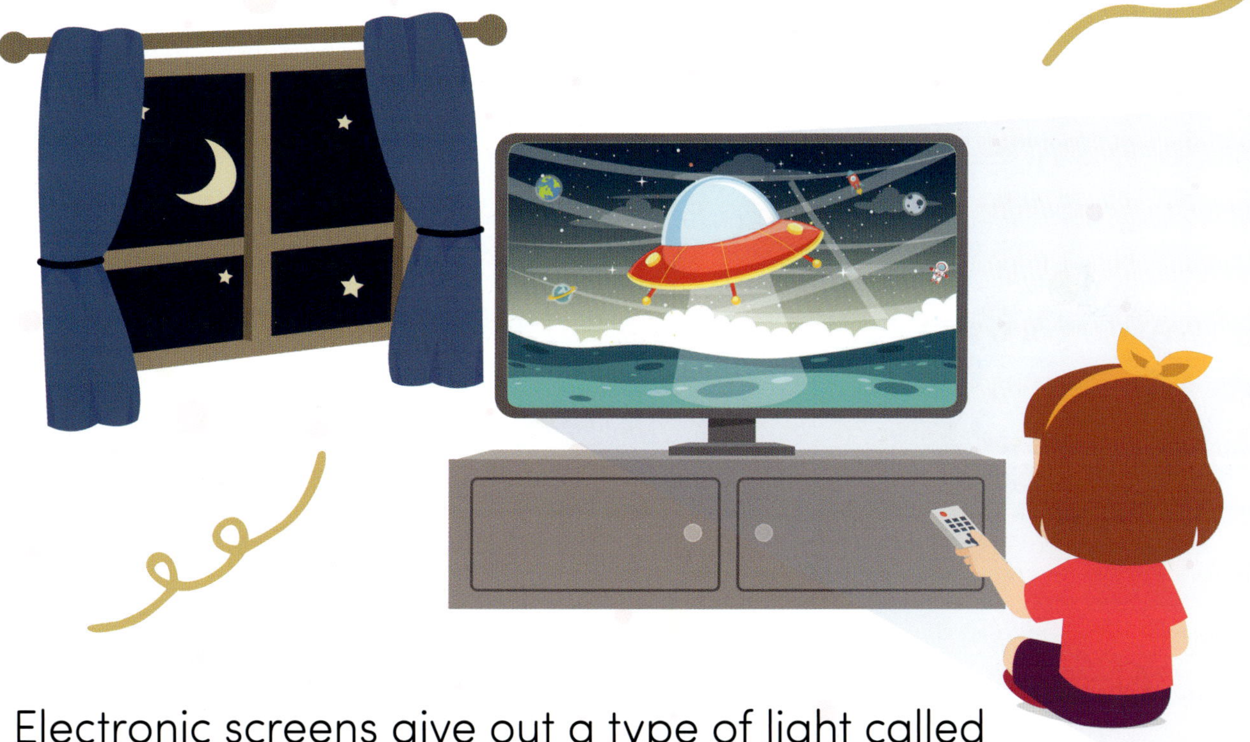

Electronic screens give out a type of light called blue light. This light can make your body produce less melatonin, making it harder to fall asleep.

Asking Questions

Asking questions is a great way to learn about the world around you. We know the answers in this book because people before you have asked the same questions.

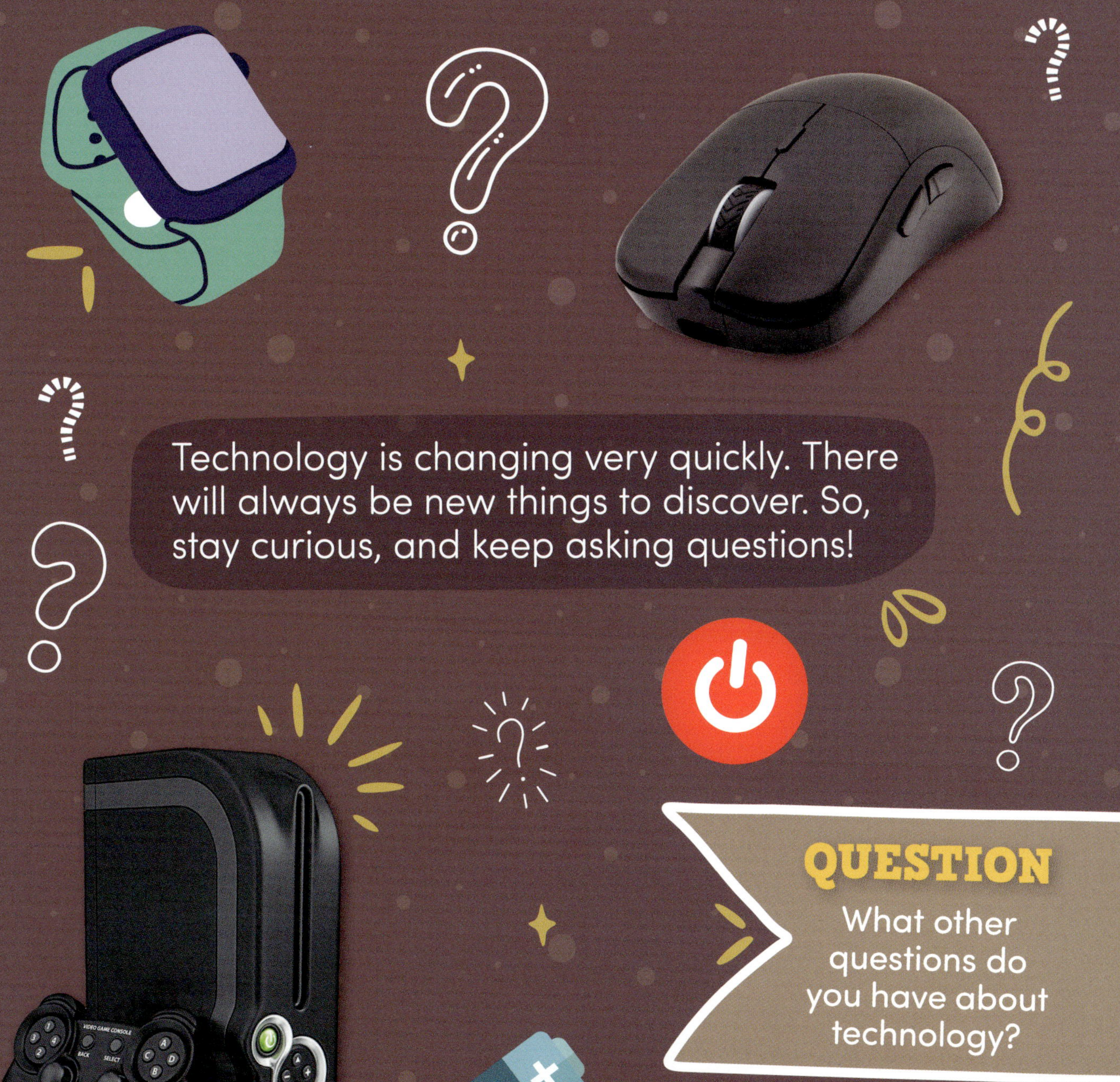

Technology is changing very quickly. There will always be new things to discover. So, stay curious, and keep asking questions!

QUESTION

What other questions do you have about technology?

Glossary

adjusting changing to make something better or more clear

damage harm

dangerous likely to cause harm or injury

devices machines such as tablets or smartphones

electricians people who work on electrical machines

electrocuted killed or seriously harmed by a strong electric shock

energy power that makes things work

fossil fuels substances, such as oil and gas, that can be burned to make energy or heat

hormone a chemical made by certain parts of the body

outlet a place where electronics are plugged in to get electricity

strain a state of stress or tiredness

voltage the force of an electrical charge as it moves in a wire or other electrical conductor

Index